The Quotable Cat

"The world of felines and their friends will be pleased to know that one of America's leading humanists has finally put together what is probably the finest international collection of jokes and humor relating to the cat (*Felis catus*). Larry Wilde, as his fans know, doesn't pussyfoot around when it comes to comedy. He has poked fun at virutally all aspects of our cultural scene and is renowned for his outrageous books of ethnic jokes. Undoubtedly the fur will fly when some of our more sensitive sisters read Mr. Wilde's often beastly (but funny) anecdotes about our precious little pets. But, overall, without being catty, I will have to say that this book succeeds marvelously at being humorous, if not hilarious, in providing a truly balanced view of the domestic cat. It may even become the catalyst so long needed to finally bring together the many alienated and distempered factions among the long- and short-haired breeds."

—Consuelo Katz
Book Review Editor,
Kitty Litter Newsletter

The NEW Official Cat Lovers Joke Book

BY Larry Wilde

PINNACLE BOOKS **NEW YORK**

THE NEW OFFICIAL CAT LOVERS JOKE BOOK

An original Pinnacle Books edition, published for the first time anywhere.

ISBN: 0-523-42004-8

First printing, March 1983

Cover illustration by Scott Ross

Printed in the United States of America

PINNACLE BOOKS, INC.
1430 Broadway
New York, New York 10018

ABOUT THE AUTHOR

Larry Wilde was born in Jersey City, New Jersey, spent two years in the U.S. Marine Corps and then graduated from the University of Miami, Florida with a Bachelor of Arts degree.

He began his career in show business as a stand-up comedian, playing the nation's nightclubs and theaters and appearing on television commercials and sitcoms like *Mary Tyler Moore, Rhoda* and *Sanford and Son*.

Mr. Wilde has published two consumate studies on the craft of comedy, *The Great Comedians* and *How The Great Comedy Writers Create Laughter*, which are considered the definitive works on that subject. He is also the author of *The Complete Book of Ethnic Humor*, the first comprehensive assortment of jokes characterizing America's mirth-loving minorities.

With sales of over 6,000,000 "Official" joke books, Mr. Wilde is now considered the world's best selling humorist. Larry and his wife, Maryruth, reside in California where he continues to write, perform, act and lecture on the subject of comedy. Mrs. Wilde recently published *The Best of Ethnic Home Cooking*.

Books by Larry Wilde

THE OFFICIAL POLISH/ITALIAN JOKE BOOK
THE OFFICIAL JEWISH/IRISH JOKE BOOK
THE OFFICIAL VIRGINS/SEX MANIACS JOKE BOOK
THE OFFICIAL BLACK FOLKS/WHITE FOLKS
  JOKE BOOK
MORE THE OFFICIAL POLISH/ITALIAN JOKE BOOK
MORE THE OFFICIAL JEWISH/IRISH JOKE BOOK
THE OFFICIAL DEMOCRAT/REPUBLICAN
  JOKE BOOK
THE OFFICIAL RELIGIOUS/NOT SO RELIGIOUS
  JOKE BOOK
THE OFFICIAL SMART KIDS/DUMB PARENTS
  JOKE BOOK
THE OFFICIAL GOLFERS JOKE BOOK
THE LAST OFFICIAL POLISH JOKE BOOK
THE OFFICIAL DIRTY JOKE BOOK
THE OFFICIAL CAT LOVERS/DOG LOVERS
  JOKE BOOK
THE LAST OFFICIAL ITALIAN JOKE BOOK
  AND
THE 1979 OFFICIAL ETHNIC CALENDAR
  ALSO
THE COMPLETE BOOK OF ETHNIC HUMOR
  (CORWIN BOOKS)
HOW THE GREAT COMEDY WRITERS CREATE
  LAUGHTER (NELSON-HALL)
THE GREAT COMEDIANS (CITADEL PRESS)

*For Fay and Milton Wildman
and their beloved Charlie.*

contents

THE *NEW*
OFFICIAL CAT LOVERS JOKE BOOK

introduction

A cat craze has been sweeping America. An estimated 34 million of these furry pets are being cuddled and cradled by cat lovers coast to coast. According to *Time,* in California you can find a cat department store, a cat dating service, a cat rest home, a cat resort, a rent-a-cat agency, cat psychics, cat acting coaches and a special annual contest to judge cats' meows.

Authors seem to have an affinity for felines. Cats belonging to Charles Dickens, Mark Twain, Lord Byron, Ernest Hemingway have been made famous by their owners. The French essayist Michel de Montaigne once made this comment:

> When I play with my cat, who knows whether I do not make her more sport than she makes me?

Quips about kittys have been making the rounds for centuries. The fun all started when those lovable four-legged creatures were brought into the home as pets. *Felis catus* was domesticated over 4,000 years ago by Egyptians who worshiped the feline as an earthly embodiment of the goddess of fertility and health.

Ever since, cat lovers have been going ga-ga over *El Gato,* but recently the fad has reached epidemic proportions. Here are some actual examples of what lengths some people will go to pamper their pets:

3

A San Francisco man listed his cat's own personal phone number in the directory in case any of his friends felt the urge to call him.

A Polish housewife was granted a divorce because her pet-loving husband shared his bed with forty-three cats and made her sleep in another room.

The owner of a Persian longhair dressed him up in top hat and tails so the cat wouldn't feel out of place at a fashionable wedding.

Felix and Morris and Mehitabel not only provide affection and companionship for their loving owners, but also made a profound contribution to our colloquial vernacular. These mouse catchers have helped stock our language with a liberal supply of colorful catchphrases:

Derisive shouts from a crowd are *catcalls*. Catching forty winks is called a *catnap*. If you step gingerly on a narrow pathway you're on a *catwalk*. When you reveal a secret you've *let the cat out of the bag*.

If you're an unimaginative imitator you're a *copycat*. If you're quick tempered and like to brawl you're a *hellcat*. If you're not a *fraidy cat*, and have *cat's eyes* to see in the dark, and want to be a thief who scales walls you'll be known as a *cat burglar*.

If you had been a devotee of jive or swing music you were a *hep cat*. Being stodgy and narrow marks you as a *heavy cat*. If you're all dressed up in the latest style, then you're a *sharp cat*. If you're also famous and have money to burn you'll be referred to as a *fat cat*.

Having a pretty face will tab you a *glamor puss*. Scowling and never smiling will stamp you as a *sourpuss*. Being dull and boring will brand you a *drizzlepuss*. If you're sour-faced and disagreeable, you'll be called a *picklepuss*.

And don't forget about *cat fights,* and *cat houses* and . . . well, you see the point. Those furry felines are going to be with us for at least another 4000 years. The affection for cats will go on as long as there is love in the world. Take a look at this:

> For months Harold had been smitten by Arlene, the new office steno. Finally he summoned up the courage to pop the question.
>
> "There are a lot of advantages to being a bachelor," he told her, "but there comes a time when one longs for the companionship of another being, a being who will regard one as perfect, as an idol; whom one can treat as one's absolute property; who will be kind and faithful when times are hard; who will share one's joys and sorrows. . . ."
>
> "Oh," said Arlene, "you're gonna buy a cat. That's great. Let me help you choose one."

If you love kittys you should be able to choose more than one of the amusing quips and gags and stories to have fun with in this collection. And take your time. You've got another 4000 years.

Larry Wilde

tabby titters

Belden swore he had a cat in his stomach and complained about it to his doctor many times. One day Belden was rushed to the hospital for an emergency appendectomy. His M.D. thought this would be a perfect opportunity to cure Belden of his cat obsession. When Belden came out of the ether the physician held up a black cat and said, "Well, we got him out of you, all right."

"You've got the wrong one," screamed Belden. "It was a white cat."

* * *

Did you hear about the cat that swallowed a ball of yarn?

Its kittens were born with angora sweaters.

Three little kittens were born to a San Diego family named Hobson. The first had one black foot. The second kitten had two black feet. The third had three black feet. So the family named them Foot, Foot Foot, and Foot Foot Foot.

One day the little Hobson girl took the kittens to the beach and tragedy struck. A wave washed one of the kittens away. The girl rushed home sobbing.

"Which one did you lose?" asked Mrs. Hobson.

"Foot," replied the girl.

"I hope you've learned your lesson," said her mother. "Don't ever take those kittens back to the beach again."

"Why not?"

"Because we've already got one Foot in the grave!"

Of a sudden the great prima donna
Cried, "Gawd, but my voice is a goner!"
   But a cat in the wings
   Said, "I know how she sings,"
And finished the solo with honor.

*   *   *

The strength of the British army is well-known throughout the world. The credit for this characteristic is given to the spinsters of Great Britain. Here's why:

The British soldier is nourished on beef; the quality of the beef is due to an abundance of clover, which is fertilized by bees. Bees can only live and multiply when protected against field mice. Field mice are kept down only if there are enough cats to catch them. Cats are the favorite pets of old maids in England.

Thus: the spinsters keep the cats that destroy the field mice, which in turn prevent the bees from being destroyed, as a consequence of which clover flourishes and the cattle grow fat and strong on clover, and the soldiers in turn grow strong because they eat the beef.

CAT

An indestructible creature provided by nature to be kicked when things go wrong in the domestic circle.

*　　*　　*

Audrey wanted to get rid of her cat but none of her friends wanted him. Marilyn, her next-door neighbor, suggested she take him into the wilderness of Los Angeles' Griffith Park and abandon him.

"He'll never find his way out of that place with its twists and windings," she said. "And someone is sure to find him and take him in."

Audrey followed her suggestion. The following week, the women met and Marilyn asked, "You got rid of your cat, didn't you?"

"No," replied Audrey. "I lost my way in the park and I had to follow the cat home."

"They demand a group rate."

A catty remark often has more lives than a cat.

*　*　*

Here lies Kitt, the cat,
Who spent many happy days;
Never known to miss a rat,
The family's pet in many ways.

*　*　*

The talented comedienne Elayne Boosier says that she never had luck with pets: "I once bought a discount cat—it was ten percent off because it came with only five lives."

Monty the mouse chanced on a pool of whiskey that was the result of a leaking barrel. Monty had had no previous experience with liquor, but now, being thirsty, he took a sip of the strange fluid, and then retired into a hole to meditate.

In a little while Monty returned to the pool, and took a second sip of whiskey. The mouse then withdrew to its hole to think some more. Presently it came out and went to the pool for the third time. Monty drank again, this time a big swallow full.

Suddenly, instead of retreating to his hole he climbed up on a soap box, stood on his hind legs, bristled his whiskers and squeaked:

"Whee! Now bring on that old cat!"

Did you hear about the cat that ate a ball of wool and had mittens?

* * *

There's a new ball-bearing type mouse-trap on the market.
It's called a Tomcat.

* * *

Then there was one vacationing tabby cat wrote to her girl friend, "Having a wonderful Tom . . . Wish you were here."

Have you heard about the thrifty tom cat that put everything he had into the kitty?

*   *   *

Last summer the book business went into a lull during the hot weather in July. The New York publishers promptly began weeping into their champagne cocktails at the Plaza Hotel. Toward the end of the month one publisher asked another, "How's business?"

"Great," he answered. "Our cat caught four mice yesterday."

Little Paul wasn't a very good altar boy. He kept making mistakes. Father Flaherty decided to give him one more chance.

"I'm performing a very difficult mass tomorrow," said the priest, "Would you like to help?"

"What do I have to do?" asked the lad.

"There's a place in the mass," said the priest, "where you'll hear me singing, 'And the angels lit the candles! All you have to do is light them. Do you think you can do that?"

"Yes sir."

On Sunday the priest went through the mass and then intoned to the congregation, "And the angels lit the candles!"

No reaction.

This time he shouted, "And the angels lit the candles."

From the back came Paul's voice. "And the cat peed on the matches!"

NEWS FLASH FROM HOLLYWOOD

Morris the Cat has retired from show business to write an advice column: Dear Tabby.

* * *

Winslow has spent the night in New England at Mrs. Kingford's Bed and Breakfast Inn. He came downstairs the next day, unable to stop yawning.

"Good morning," said the owner cheerfully.

"Good morning," he answered.

"What's the matter, didn't you sleep well?"

"No, I didn't. Your cat kept me awake all night."

"Oh," said Mrs. Kingford defiantly, "I suppose you think I oughta have the poor thing killed."

"No," said the traveler, "But would you mind having it tuned?"

"I heard you got a new cat."

"Yeah, they claimed he was a Siamese—but he can't speak one word of Siamese."

*　　*　　*

"I wanted to call my cat Napoleon but my mother wouldn't let me. She said it would be an insult to the man. Then I wanted to name him after you, but my mother wouldn't let me."

"Good for her."

"She said it would be an insult to the cat."

Flanagan weaved and bobbed his way into a saloon and shouted, "Does anyone here . . . hic . . . own a large black cat with a white . . . hic . . . collar?"

There was no reply.

"Hey," stammered the Irishman, "does anybody here own a big black cat with a white collar?"

There was silence in the saloon.

"Oh, my God!" sobbed Flanagan, "I must've run over a priest."

* * *

Little Loretta ran to her father and sobbed, "Mommy just drowned one of my kittens."

"That's too bad, sweetheart," he comforted, "but maybe she had to do it!"

"No, she didn't," said the girl, "she promised I could."

Many people are like cats. They lick themselves with their tongues.

* * *

FELINE PHILOSOPHY

When the cat's away, empty the litter box.

* * *

Mrs. Greene entered a Chicago department store and said she wanted to knit a sweater for her cat. "What size?" asked the salesgirl.

"I really don't know," said the woman. "I have her out in the car."

"Why don't you bring the cat in here so we can measure her?" suggested the girl.

"Oh, I couldn't do that," replied the horrified customer. "You see, this sweater is to be a surprise!"

Forsythe and Wentworth, two British archeologists, were digging in an Egyptian tomb when they came upon a tiny pile of fresh feces.

"Good heavens," exclaimed Forsythe, "do you think possibly a cat crept into the crypt, crapped and crept out again?"

"No," replied Wentworth, the confirmed cat lover. "I think it was a pup that popped into the pit, pooped and then popped out."

*　　*　　*

NEWSPAPER WANT AD

Attractive kitten seeks position
purring in a nice little girl's
lap. Will also do light mouse
　　　　　　　　work.

What does an 85-pound canary say? "Here, kitty, kitty . . . !"

* * *

Hostess: Our cat is just like one of the family.
Guest: Yes. I can see the resemblance.

* * *

Did you hear about the young Baltimore bachelor who paid careful attention to his rich old aunt and was especially affectionate to the eight cats she loved?

When the old lady died, she willed the eight cats to her nephew.

A Presbyterian minister, awarding prizes at a cat show, was scandalized at the outfits worn by some of the women.

"Look at that youngster," said the clergyman, "The one with the cropped hair, the cigarette, jeans, holding two Persian cats. Is it a boy or a girl?"

"A girl," said his companion. "She's my daughter."

"My dear sir," said the flustered minister, "Please forgive me, I would never have been so outspoken had I known you were her father."

"I'm not," said the other, "I'm her mother."

Miss Priscilla, an old maid, was chatting with her neighbor. "I'm going to enter Anthony in the cat show next month."

"Do you think he'll win many prizes?" asked the neighbor.

"No," said the spinster, "but he'll meet some very nice cats."

*　*　*

You all know the Countess of Bray
And you'll hardly believe when I say,
　That in spite of her station,
　Birth, rank, education,
She always spelled "cat" with a "K".

Mrs. Bostwick's cat Timmy had died. He had been like a son to the woman and she wanted to have an elaborate burial ceremony. Mrs. Bostwick went to a nearby Protestant church to make the arrangements.

"I'm sorry," said the minister, "but it would be blasphemous to bestow upon a cat the solemn ritual we offer a human being. But this may not be the view that all men take. Try the synagogue down the street."

The rabbi was even more discouraging. "You must understand," he explained, "that a cat is ritually unclean. Why don't you try the Catholic church. Maybe they can help you."

Father MacCready listened carefully and then shook his head. "I appreciate your feelings, but it cannot be done."

"Well, Father, if it can't be, it can't be," said the distraught woman. "I was prepared to donate $10,000 to any church that took care of my little Timmy."

"One moment, my daughter," said the priest. "Did I understand you to say that the cat was a Catholic?"

cat-a-logues

"Is it really bad luck to have a black cat cross your path?"

"Well, it depends on whether you're a man or a mouse."

*   *   *

The wealthy tourist lost his prized blue-eyed white Persian while stopping over in a tiny New England town. He quickly inserted an ad in the local newspaper offering a $100 reward.

The next day he dialed the newspaper office to inquire, but found no one there but an old janitor.

"Where's the newspaper staff?" asked the man.

"They're all out," said the janitor, "trying to find that cat of yours."

Ned: Didn't you know that black cats are unlucky?

Ed: This one isn't. He just ate your dinner.

*   *   *

Farrell and Donelson met on the street.

"Hey," said Farrell, "remember that $5 check you gave me for drowning your cat?"

"Yeah," replied Donelson. "What about it?"

"It came back."

"So did the cat."

CAT

*An animal that never cries
over spilled milk*

*   *   *

Lovely Rosanna Lopez, the lightning force behind New York's Celebrity Bulletin, loves this lulu:

Ted and Bob, two high school seniors, were having a Coke. "Your grandfather's a little deaf, isn't he?" asked Ted.

"A *little* deaf?" replied Bob. "Yesterday, he said his prayers kneeling on the cat!"

There once were two cats in Kilkenny.
Each thought there was one cat too many.
　And they scratched and they fit,
　And they tore and they bit,
'Till instead of two cats—there weren't any.

* 　 * 　 *

"The cat is a wonderful animal, just as clean as a whistle."

"Oh, cats aren't so clean."

"Don't argue with me. Cats are very clean. Take a look at the little pussy in the corner. It's always washing its face."

"I don't know about that. Cats don't wash their faces. They wash their feet and wipe them on their faces."

* 　 * 　 *

SIGN IN PET SHOP

Attention Cat Lovers! Save Money!
Feed your cat lox. Instead of cream
they'll drink water!

Elaine Partnow, author of The Quotable Woman, a magnificent collection of thoughts expressed by famous ladies, loves this lollapalooza:

Linwood, an antique dealer, noticed a mangy little kitten lapping up milk from a saucer in front of Dubin's Delicatessen. He recognized the saucer as being a rare and precious piece of pottery.

Just then Dubin came out. Linwood offered $5 for the cat.

"It's not for sale," said Dubin.

"Look," said the antique connoisseur, "that cat is dirty and undesirable, but I'm eccentric. I like cats that way. I'll give you ten dollars."

"It's a deal," said Dubin.

"For that much money I'm sure you won't mind throwing in the saucer," said Linwood. "The kitten seems so happy drinking from it."

"Nothing doing," said Dubin. "That's my lucky saucer. From that saucer, so far this week, I've sold thirty-eight cats."

Dennis Pinney, the terrific Pacific telephone repair specialist, tells this tempestuous titillator:

Henderson knocked on the farmhouse door and a white-haired lady opened it.

"Excuse me," said Henderson, "do you own a calico cat with a red collar and a silver bell attached to it?"

"Yes," said the elderly woman, "that's my cat."

"Well, I just ran over it," explained the man. "I'm terribly sorry. Of course, I'll replace him."

"Then just don't stand there," replied the old lady. "There's a mouse in the kitchen!"

"Eight years to get me to talk and then he
doesn't listen."

Harper inserted a classified ad in a local newspaper offering a $100 reward for the return—no question asked—of his wife's pet cat.

"That's a mighty big reward for a cat," said the clerk accepting the ad.

"Not for this one," said Harper. "I drowned it."

* * *

There was a kind curate of Kew
Who kept a large cat in a pew;
There he taught it each week
A new letter of Greek,
But it never got further than "Mu."

Mrs. Fletcher walked in front of her husband and turned off the television set.

"Hey, what are you doing?" he shouted.

"My mother won't stay in this house another moment," announced Mrs. Fletcher, "unless we get rid of the mice."

Mr. Fletcher leaped out of his chair and headed for the door.

"Where are you going?" shouted his wife.

"To get rid of the cat."

* * *

Comedian Albert Bernie was reminiscing about his youth on the lower East Side of New York:

"My neighborhood was so tough—any cat with a tail was a tourist."

David, a student at Michigan, received a telephone call from his brother Blake back home.

"Hi, David," said Blake, "Your cat's dead."

David fell apart. He began crying uncontrollably. When, finally, he was able to compose himself, he scolded his brother.

"Dammit, Blake," he told him. "You know how I loved that cat. You didn't have to call me and just spill it out, first thing—'your cat's dead.' You should have broken it to me gently. You could have said: 'Dave, the cat got out the window the other day and crawled up the rainspout and got up on the roof and slipped and fell," and then you could have said it died."

"I'm sorry," apologized Blake.

"Okay, forget it," said David. "How's Mom?"

"Well, Mom got out the window the other day and crawled up the rainspout . . ."

Did you hear about the puss in Meowi,
Florida, who ate cheese so he could peer
down ratholes with baited breath?

*　　*　　*

A mouse in her room woke Miss Dowd.
She was frightened—it must be allowed.
  Soon a happy thought hit her—
  To scare off the critter,
She sat up in bed and meowed.

Irwin Zucker, America's foremost book publicist, breaks up buddies with this belly-laugh:

Morgan telephoned his doctor frantically in the middle of the night.

"Come quick. You know my wife always sleeps with her mouth wide open. Well, just now a mouse ran down her throat."

"I'll be over in a few minutes," said the doctor. "Meanwhile, try waving a piece of cheese in front of her mouth and maybe the mouse will come out."

When the M.D. arrived, he found Morgan in his pajamas waving a six-pound flounder frantically in front of his wife's face.

"What's the idea?" said the exasperated doctor, "I told you to wave a piece of cheese. Mice don't like flounders.

"I know," gasped Morgan. "But first we've got to get the cat out."

Lieutenant Berry got a pass for his wife and daughter to visit him at the camp. The two went around to the side gate, which was the shortest route to his headquarters.

But a sentry stopped them. "Sorry, but you'll have to go in through the front gate," he said. "I've got orders nobody is allowed to pass through here."

"But we're the Berrys," protested the mother.

"Lady, I don't care if you're the cat's pajamas—you can't go through this gate."

*　　*　　*

"I heard you have a cat that can say her own name."

"That's right."

"What's her name?"

"Meow!"

Mary Staton, brilliant sci-fi author of From the Legend of Biel, tells about newly married Marge, who wept when her husband came home:

"Oh," she sobbed. "I baked a cake and the cat ate it all up."

"Don't worry dear," he replied. "I'll get you a new cat."

*　　*　　*

A new book on cats hit the bookstalls and in one Cleveland store became an immediate bestseller. The owner sold his entire stock in two hours and reordered 100 more copies. The publisher wired:

100 CATS ON THE WAY. ARE YOUR CUSTOMERS MICE OR MEN?

The visitor to New York rushed from the airport into a waiting taxi, trying to keep dry in the heavy downpour.

"Can you think of anything worse," grumbled the visitor, "than raining cats and dogs in New York?"

"Sure," said the cab driver. "Hailing taxis!"

*   *   *

The butcher was busy waiting on a woman when Mrs. Higgins rushed in and said, "Give me a pound of cat food, quick!"

Turning to the other customer, who had been waiting for some time, Mrs. Higgins said: "I hope you don't mind my getting waited on before you."

"Not if you're that hungry," replied the other woman.

Rick Friedberg, Hollywood's top cinematographer-director, dreamed up this doozy:

Two neighbors, Welch and Dyer, were chatting over their back fence. "I've got mice overrunning the house," complained Welch.

"Why don't you get a cat?" suggested Dyer.

"That's a good idea," said Welch. "I'll stop at the pet shop on my way home and buy one."

A few weeks later Dyer dropped in on Welch for a visit. He was taken down to the cellar to have a look at the new cat.

"Holy smoke!" exclaimed Dyer. "What kind of a cat is that? He's playing with the mice."

"Sure," said Welch. "Those are our mice. But you let a strange mouse stick his nose in here and you'll see some action."

"If a strange mouse gets in here,
then you'll see some action!"

Stories about Yogi Berra's antics while a member of the New York Yankees are legion. This one is sworm to by a couple of Yogi's teammates:

One night the stocky catcher was horrified to see a small kitten toppling from the branches of a tree across the way from him. He dashed over and made a miraculous catch—but the force of habit proved too much for him. He straightened up and threw the cat to second base.

*   *   *

CATACOMB

An implement for grooming cats

Mrs. Cronin, a sour-faced dowager, was riding a Manhattan subway train heading toward the Bronx. A man sat opposite her calmly reading his newspaper with three kittens resting peacefully on his lap. Mrs. Cronin contemplated the situation until she could stand it no longer. She tapped on his paper and said, "Pardon me, but what on earth are you doing with those cats in the subway?"

"Them?" said the man. "I really don't know, lady. They must have gotten on at 59th Street."

Stalin was giving Mao Tse Tung instructions in practical Communism.

"Comrade," he said, "how would you make a cat eat chili pepper?"

"There are two ways," said Mao. "I could force it down him, or I could stuff a fish with the pepper and give the fish to the cat."

"Wrong," replied Stalin. "It's not compatible with our ideology. The first method is coercion, the second deception. You know we never coerce or deceive the people."

"Then how would you do it?" asked Mao.

"I would rub the pepper on the cat's tail. When this started to smart, the cat would turn around and lick its tail, thus eating the pepper voluntarily."

Zetta Castle, the pretty La Costa Country Club publicity lady who put that fabulous playland on the map, pitched this poignant pearl:

Old Nugent loved his cat, Tommy, so dearly he tried to teach it to talk. "If I can get Tommy to converse with me," he reasoned, "I won't have to bother with ornery humans at all."

First he tried a diet of canned salmon, then one of canaries. Tommy liked both—but he didn't learn to talk. Then one day Nugent had two extremely talkative parrots cooked in butter and served to Tommy with asparagus and French fries. Tommy licked the plate clean, and then—wonder of wonders—suddenly turned to his master and shouted, "Look out!"

Nugent didn't move. The ceiling caved in and buried the old man under a mass of debris. Tommy shook his head and said, "Eight years he spends getting me to talk, and then the dummy doesn't listen."

Steve Martin, one of the brightest of the new comedy stars, convulses audiences with these comic cat observations:

"Heard you weren't supposed to give cats baths but my cat came home and he was really dirty. So I decided to give him a bath and it was great. He just sat there. He enjoyed it. It was fun for me. The fur would stick to my tongue but other than that . . ."

*　　*　　*

FELINE PHILOSOPHY

It is better to have your path crossed by a black cat than by a Mack truck

In an East Berlin schoolroom, little Hans was asked to give an example of a dependent clause.

"Our cat has a litter of ten kittens," he replied, "all of which are good Communists."

"That's excellent," said the teacher. "You have a good grasp on grammar as well as the Party Line."

The following week the government inspector visited the school and the teacher called on Hans.

"Our cat has a litter of ten kittens," said Hans, "all of which are good Western Democrats."

"That is not what you said a week ago!" snapped the teacher.

"Yes," replied Hans, "but my kittens' eyes are open now."

Morey Amsterdam, a great comedian and one of the best loved members of the show business profession, tells this wisp of whimsy:

Many years ago in a small town in Europe a cat accidently had its leg amputated. The major ordered it put away but a wood carver offered to take the animal.

He built a wooden leg for the cat and soon it was getting around perfectly. Very soon it became the talk of the town, for the cat each day wandered off into the woods and killed wolves.

"How can that little three-legged cat kill wolves?" the people asked the wood carver.

"Very simply," he replied. "The cat climbs all over them with the three good legs and then beats them to death with the wooden one!"

kits and kids

Five-year-old Bobby sat on the front porch holding his cat. A little girl who lived around the corner approached him and said, "What's your cat's name?"

"Ben Hur," replied the little boy.

"How did you happen to call it that?"

"We used to call it Ben—until it had kittens."

*   *   *

What do you call a cat that robs Mac-Donald's?"

A cat burger-lar.

"Walter!" exclaimed the shocked mother, "You mustn't pull the cat's tail!"

"I'm not pulling the cat's tail!" shouted Walter. "I'm standing on it and he's doin' all the pullin'!"

*　*　*

Young Richard was ordered to bring in the cats one evening, and there followed a crescendo of meowing and spitting. "What are you doing to those poor cats?" demanded Richard's mother.

"Nothing at all," said the boy, "I'm being especially careful. I'm carrying them by their stems."

"Did you put the cat out?"
"Why? Is it on fire?"

*   *   *

Laura Milligan, whose mom, Joyce, is the popular San Jose Mercury News correspondent, came up with this cutie:

"What did one cat say to the other?"

"I don't know."

"I don't know either. But if you see two cats talking, come get me quick."

CAT

A miniature tiger kept in a home
to remind children to wash their
faces

*   *   *

Mother: Why are you feeding the cat bird-
             seed?
Daughter: That's where my bird is.

*   *   *

"Can you name four members of the cat family?"
"The father, the mother, and two kittens."

Little Teddy had never seen a cat with her litter. He watched for a while and then ran excitedly to his aunt's bedroom. "Come quick, Aunt Marion," he cried. "There's a great big kitty lying on the floor and five little kitties are blowing her up!"

*   *   *

"Did you ever see the Catskill Mountains?"
"No, but I've seen them kill mice."

*   *   *

"Have you ever seen a catfish?"
"Of course."
"How did he hold the pole?"

"Spell the word cat."
"C . . . A . . ."
"But what's at the end of it?"
"A tail."

*   *   *

Why did the cat join the Red Cross?
She wanted to be a first aid kit.

*   *   *

What do you call a fat cat?
A flabby tabby.

Angelic Angela Lewerke amuses the St. Brendan pupils with this agreeable anecdote:

Four-year-old Jimmy was stroking his cat before the fireplace in perfect content. The cat, also happy, began to purr loudly. Jimmy gazed at her and then suddenly seized the cat by the tail and dragged her roughly from the hearth.

"You mustn't hurt your kitty," said his mother.

"I'm not," said Jimmy, "but I've got to get her away from the fire. She's beginning to boil."

Ann Marchiony, California's top-notch publicity lady, chuckles over this little charmer:

"Mama!" shouted little Paul from the living room. "Come quick!"

"What is it, son?"

"The cat has gone to sleep and left its motor running."

"It's your father. I'd know that
voice anywhere!"

What do you call ten cats walking down an alley?

A pussy posse.

* * *

Payne and his young son boarded a bus and took a seat behind the driver. The youngster was carrying a covered box with obvious pride.

"Daddy," he asked, "is my new kitten a man kitten or a lady kitten?"

"A man kitten."

"How do you know?"

The other passengers listened to hear his answer.

"Because," answered the father, "he has whiskers."

What makes more noise than a cat stuck in a tree?
Two cats stuck in a tree.

*   *   *

Why does a cat scratch himself?
He's the only one that knows where it itches.

*   *   *

What does a cat do when it hears a mouse squeak?
Oils it.

What did the cat say as he ran through the screen door?

"I feel strained."

*   *   *

What is the difference between a cat and a comma?"

A cat has claws at the end of its paws, but a comma has a pause at the end of its clause.

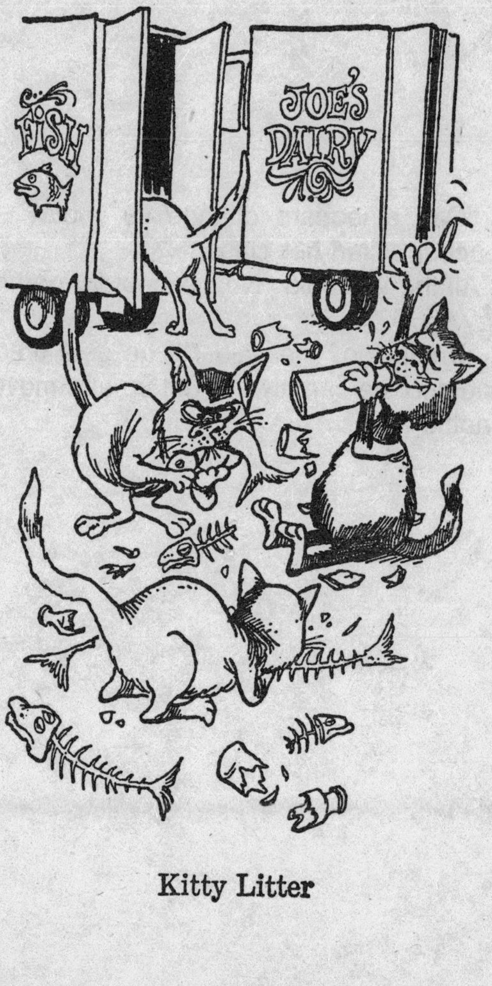
FISH
JOE'S
DAIRY

Kitty Litter

What is four feet on four feet waiting for four feet?

A cat on a chair waiting for a mouse.

* * *

"Can a leopard change its spots?" the teacher asked her class.

All the tots said "No," except for one little boy.

"It can too," he said. "If he gets tired of one spot he can always get up and move to another."

What do they call a cat who crossed the Sahara?
Sandy Claws.

*   *   *

Which side of a cat has the most fur?
The outside.

*   *   *

What time is it when twelve dogs chase a cat?
Twelve after one.

Billy, a grammar school pupil, handed in this composition on cats:

Cats thats meant for little boys to maul and tease is called Maultease cats. Some cats is rekernized by how quiet their purr is and these is Purrsian cats. Cats what has bad tempers is named Angora cats. And cats with deep feelings is called Felines. I don't like cats.

What would you call a small black cat in Russia if it was ten days old and had a white spot on the end of its nose?
A kitten.

* * *

Why do kittens make good television announcers?
Because they have wee paws for station identification.

* * *

What does a cat have that a dog doesn't?
Kittens.

What did the cat say when his tail got caught in the lawnmower?
"It won't be long now."

*　　*　　*

"My cat can count."
"Really?"
"I asked her what two minus two was and she said nothing."

"How can you tell if a cat is a male or a female?"

"I don't know."

"Tell it a joke. If he laughs it's a male. If she laughs, it's a female."

* * *

What never was and never will be?
A mouse's nest in a cat's ear.

* * *

If ten copycats were sitting on a fence and one jumped off, how many would be left?

None, because they are copycats.

Where did the three little kittens find their mittens?

In the Yellow Pages.

* * *

Teacher: Mary, can you make up a sentence with the phrase "bitter end" in it?

Mary: How about "Our dog chased our cat, and he bitter end."

Why is a cat bigger at night than it is in the morning?

Because it is let out at night and taken in in the morning.

*   *   *

What happens when you give a cat lemons?

You get a sourpuss.

Heather Hewitt, the lovely Hollywood model/actress, tells about the two neighborhood youngsters who stopped her on the way home:

"Lady," said one lad, "if you give us a quarter, my little brother will imitate a cat."

"What will he do?" asked Heather. "Meow?"

"No," answered the boy. "He wouldn't do a cheap imitation like that. He'll eat a mouse."

What do you get when you cross a cat with a laughing hyena?

A giggle puss.

* * *

What's better than a talking cat?
A spelling bee.

* * *

Where was the yellow cat when the lights went out?

In the dark.

What's a cat's skin used for?
To keep the cat inside.

*　　*　　*

"When I bought this cat, you told me he was good for mice. He doesn't catch any."
"Well, isn't that good for mice?"

*　　*　　*

"My cat swallowed a flashlight."
"Did it make him sick?"
"No, he hiccuped with delight."

"My cat ate a whole ball of wool."

"So what?"

"So her kittens were all born wearing sweaters."

"That's some yarn."

"Well, I'm a knit-wit."

*   *   *

"Why is your cat so small?"

"I feed him condensed milk."

*   *   *

Little Richie ran into the kitchen and shouted, "Oh Mommy, look! There's a big cat standing outside, it's as big as a house!"

"Richard, why do you exaggerate!" exclaimed his mother. "I've told you twenty million times about that habit of yours."

crazy cats

A mouse and a cat walked into a restaurant and sat down. The mouse ordered three kinds of cheese and some grain. The waiter asked what the cat would like, and the mouse answered that the cat wanted nothing.

"Is something the matter?" asked the waiter.

"Hey, if he were hungry," snapped the mouse, "do you think I'd be sitting here?"

Two cats were watching a tennis match. One turned to the other and said, "You know, my father is in that racket."

*   *   *

CAT

A pet who sleeps away
A goodly portion of the day
So he can prowl and fight
When we would like to sleep at night.
                              —Richard Wheeler

Mamma cat was scolding one of her kittens for coming home late and kitty said, "Can't I lead one of my own lives?"

* * *

A big, mangy dog was threatening a mother cat and her kittens. He had backed them into a corner of a barn, when suddenly the cat reared back on her hind legs and started barking and growling loudly. Startled and confused, the dog turned and ran from the barn, its tail tucked between its legs.

Turning to her kittens, the mother cat lifted a paw and told them: "Now do you see the advantage of being bilingual?"

"That's a beautiful stuffed tiger you've got there. Where did you get him?"

"In India, when I was on a hunting expedition with my uncle."

"What's he stuffed with?"

"My uncle."

*   *   *

While hunting in the woods one afternoon, the old mountaineer was surprised by a wildcat that chased him to the top limbs of a large oak tree that overhung the edge of a deep canyon.

The wildcat was climbing as fast as the man and soon had forced him perilously near the end of a dead limb extending far out over the canyon. The mountaineer decided it was time to do some talking.

"Listen, varmint," he said. "If you make me move one inch farther, you're going to have to jump a hell of a long ways for your supper."

"Let that be a lesson to you—keep away
from Blumberg's Fur Shop."

There was a young lady of Niger,
Who smiled as she rode on a tiger.
   They returned from the ride
   With the lady inside,
And the smile on the face of the tiger.

Spinster Peabody's proudest possession was Count, her exquisite calico. Unfortunately, he had been missing for two days. When she opened the freezer door, Miss Peabody nearly died of shock. There was Count frozen solid.

She immediately called the vet, who said there still might be a chance to save the poor animal.

"Give it two tablespoons of gasoline," he told her.

With trembling hands, Miss Peabody opened Count's mouth and carefully spooned in the doctor's strange prescription.

The seconds ticked away and nothing happened. She was about to give up hope when suddenly, the cat opened his eyes, let out an ear-piercing screech and shot across the room at a hundred miles per hour, running over the furniture, the walls, even the ceiling. Count kept this up for two minutes and then suddenly stopped dead in his tracks, not moving a muscle.

Miss Peabody called the vet again. "What do you think happened?" she asked.

"Simple," said the doctor. "He ran out of gas."

Glenn Speidel, the munificent mogul of Hollywood General Studios, broke up a party with this peerless pun:

During the days when Roy Rogers and Dale Evans were America's Singing Sweethearts, Roy was out walking near their ranch. Suddenly, he was attached by a wildcat and the animal tore apart Rogers' brand new boots.

Roy rushed back to the ranch. "Look," he exclaimed to Dale, "what that wildcat did to my new boots!"

"Ah, that's a shame!" said Dale. Roy grabbed his shotgun and announced, "I'm gonna get that cat!"

Rogers tracked the animal, killed it, threw it over his shoulder, and marched triumphantly to the ranch. Dale saw what her husband was carrying and she sang:

"Pardon me, Roy, is that the cat that chewed you boot shoes?"

Did you hear about the tiger who cornered Mr. Aesop, and then proceeded to eat him for his Sunday dinner?

"Go ahead, Aesop," said the tiger, "try and make up a fable about this!"

*   *   *

Little Sheldon seemed to be enjoying himself at the zoo with his father. As they were looking at the tigers, however, a troubled look came over the boy's face. His father asked him what was the matter.

"I was just wondering, Daddy. In case a tiger breaks loose and eats you, what number bus do I take home?"

A group of hikers passing a hillbilly's cabin smiled as they saw the owner reclining in a rocking chair on the porch. They noticed his wife going into the house via the front and only door and a few seconds later saw a wildcat leap through the open window.

They rushed up to the moutaineer. "Do something quick!" someone shouted. "A wildcat just leaped into your house and your wife is in there."

"That's his tough luck," said the hillbilly, "I never did like wildcats, anyway."

"That sure hit the spot," said the leopard after he'd eaten the hunter.

* * *

There was a young man from the city
Who met what he thought was a kitty.
  He gave it a pat
  And said "Nice little cat."
They buried his clothes, out of pity.

cool cats

Bob Harlon, boss of the armed forces radio and TV network in Europe, had a cat in his Frankfurt home that snoozed unconcernedly in the sun while dozens of mice scurried happily by. Harlon finally gave up on the cat and bought a mouse trap. Its first victim was the cat.

Letting the cat out of the bag is much easier than putting it back.

Jocular Jim Parrish, of Darby Pest Control, likes this jolly jest:

On one of his pastoral visits, a minister noticed fifteen holes cut in a door and inquired what they were for.

"We have fifteen cats, and that's for them to go out through," the man of the house explained.

"Well, why do you need fifteen holes? Can't they all go out through the same hole one by one?" questioned the minister.

"Friend," said the fellow, "when my wife says 'scat,' she means it!"

Ex-president and Mrs. Gerald Ford have a lovely estate in Palm Springs and also a prize Siamese they named Burt Reynolds.

Last winter a jokester sent a postcard addressed to Burt Reynolds, c/o the Fords. An alert real estate promoter spotted the card at the post office and figured that he had a hot prospect to work on. He rushed over to the Fords and demanded to see Burt immediately. "He must be around somewhere," said an obliging maid, "Here, Burt, here!"

Another Ford, Tennessee Ernie to be exact, managed to maintain his great public acceptance by virtue of a pleasing voice and a pleasant personality. Ernie also developed a reputation for his colorful quips. Here's a line he ad-libbed on an opening night in Las Vegas:

"I'm as nervous as a long-tailed cat in a room full of rocking chairs."

CATEGORY

Scary tales for scaredy-cats

*   *   *

President Coolidge once invited some Vermont friends to the White House. Being unfamiliar with protocol, his guests determined to do whatever the President did. During dinner, they watched him carefully—but were astounded when coffee was served and Coolidge poured his into a saucer. Shrugging, the guests followed suit. Coolidge added sugar and cream. So they did also.

Then Coolidge leaned over and gave his saucer to the White House cat.

Guthrie Kraut, the genial California golf book dispenser, bounces Bingo, his beautiful Burmese while delivering this dash of drollery:

Miss Edmonds, the fifth grade teacher, was surprised to see only one child in class on the first day of a rural school. She was aghast when the little pupil told her that the others were throwing cats into the river.

A few minutes later, another child wandered into class. "Why are you tardy?" asked Miss Edwards.

"I was throwin' cats in the river," he replied.

"That's awful!" she gasped. "How could you do such a thing!"

One by one the other boys wandered into class, all with the same excuse.

Finally the smallest pupil of all arrived.

"Why are you late?" demanded the teacher. "Were you throwing cats into the river, too?"

"No," said the little boy, "I'm Katz!"

Comedian Rodney Dangerfield likes to include this plum at his personal appearances:

"My childhood was so rough I had to share my sandbox with a cat."

*   *   *

Israeli wits swear to the authenticity of this story. Seems there was a meeting between King Faisal and David Ben-Gurion in Saudi Arabia. "Just look at all those gushing oil wells," boasted Faisal. "Isn't this a marvelous country?"

"Your Highness," answered the great Jewish leader, "if it weren't for those wells, all you have is a million square miles of kitty litter."

Jackie Gayle, the best of the newer funny men, cracked up a Beverly Hills banquet with:

"I'll never forget the day I landed in California. The sun was shining cats and dogs."

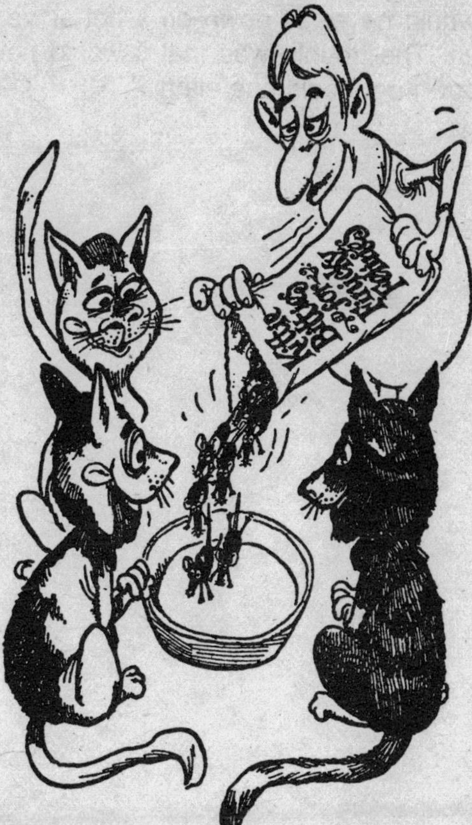
Kitty Bits
for
Finicky
Felines

Perhaps America's greatest humorist, Mark Twain, used to say that it was possible to learn too much from experience. "A cat," he said, "that had squatted once on a hot stove lid would never sit down on a hot stove lid again. The trouble was that it would never sit down on a cold one either."

Sam Levinson has entertained millions with his warm, down-to-earth comedy. This talented humorist is especially funny when talking about his family and early childhood. Here are a couple of samples:

"When I was little, I had a cat named Hamlin who specialized in getting in my mother's way. Sometimes at night, in the dark, Mama would step on Hamlin's paws, and when the cat howled she would say in self-defense, "Who tells it to walk around barefoot?"

My mama and papa above all else, wanted that their children be "cultured," but they couldn't quite cope with the textbooks we kids brought home from public school. "I read here," complained Papa one day, "that the cow says, 'Moo, Moo,' the dog says, 'Woof, Woof,' the cat says 'Meow'—what's the matter with these animals? Can't they speak English?"

One night at a Friars Roast, Jack Benny kidded George Jessel because George was constantly being called upon to deliver eulogies.

"One of the nicest eulogies I ever heard Jessel deliver," quipped Benny, "was for one of James Mason's cats. When Jessel finished eulogizing the cat there wasn't a dry eye in the house. You just wouldn't believe what that cat had done for Israel and the Democrats."

Fred Allen, a close friend of the James Masons, was dining one night at the home of Mary and Jack Benny. "Fred, you're sitting at my usual place at the table," said Mary, "so will you please fish under your chair for the buzzer to summon the butler? Then tell me what your friends the Masons do with all those cats around the house."

"For one thing," answered Allen, "they never have to hunt for a buzzer. They just step on one of the cats."

THE MOST OUTRAGEOUS HUMOR
BOOK EVER PUBLISHED!

101 USES
FOR THE
UNEMPLOYED

by Neuman and Neuman

☐ 41-990-2 **101 USES FOR THE UNEMPLOYED** $2.50

Buy it at your local bookstore or use this handy coupon
Clip and mail this page with your order